THIS JOURNAL BELONGS TO

____

BE STRONG AND COURAGEOUS. DO NOT FEAR OR BE IN DREAD OF THEM, FOR IT IS THE LORD YOUR GOD WHO GOES WITH YOU. HE WILL NOT LEAVE YOU OR FORSAKE YOU.

DEUTERONOMY 31:6

MESSAGE US ON INSTAGRAM

@bluebelovedco

SEND US YOUR CODE "WK287" AND WE WILL SEND YOU

SOME FREEBIES!

Do you have a need in your life and would like someone to stand in faith with you? Send us your prayer requests on Instagram or email us at *bluebelovedco@gmail.com* and we would love to pray with you.

"For where two or three are gathered in my name, there am I among them."

- MATTHEW 18:20

Weak Made Strong

Publisher: Blue Beloved Co | Author: Rev. Samuel Day | Illustrator: by Chia P.

For wholesale inquiries please contact: bluebelovedco@gmail.com

CONTENTS

EPHESIANS 3:17

SO THAT CHRIST MAY DWELL IN YOUR HEARTS THROUGH FAITH—THAT YOU, BEING

rooted and grounded in love

ANCHORED IN LOVE

EPHESIANS 3:17

The Apostle Paul reminds us that Daddy God did not just send His Son to deliver us from all our sins. Our sinful mindset, the world and Satan will often remind us of all our past failures and sins. However, Father God's intention is not only for us to be delivered from sins but also to live in the fullness of God! What is the key? To be rooted and grounded in God's love. To know His love that goes beyond our natural understanding. This comes as we meditate on the extent of The Father's love shown through the sacrifice of His Son on the cross.

REFLECTION

Why is being rooted and grounded in God's love important? A good way to reflect is to understand why trees need good roots. What purpose do those roots have? Consider the storms the trees face with our "storms".

Christ has delivered us from the power of sin and our past. How does that make you feel?

You are destined to be filled with the fullness of God. Why is that so important to know?

NOTES

*EXTRA SPACE FOR SECTION 2 REFLECTION, SERMON NOTES, AND OTHERS

PRAYER REQUEST

Abba Father, we declare and sing, this is the day that You have made, and we will rejoice and be glad in it. We enter into Your gates with thanksgiving and into Your courts with praise. We are highly favored, incredibly blessed, and deeply loved. In Jesus Name. Amen.

PERSONAL	OTHERS

AFFIRMATION
& GRATITUDE

1.

2.

3.

THINGS ON MY HEART

HIGHLIGHTS

TEACH ME | GUIDE ME

FROM HIS MOUTH COME KNOWLEDGE AND UNDERSTANDING;

PROVERBS 2:6

THE X FACTOR PROVERBS 2:6

What would it be if God asked you to ask for anything you would like? This proverb is written by King Solomon, who is thought to be the most successful king in the history of Israel. When God told him he could ask for anything, he asked for wisdom. We are often told that knowledge and understanding empower us to succeed in every area of life. However, this alone is not enough. The X factor for great success is how we put knowledge and understanding to use. This is called wisdom. The Lord alone is the true source of wisdom. When we have wisdom, we can steward everything God gives us. Without wisdom, we cannot hold on to anything.

REFLECTION

Daddy God is the source of all wisdom. What do you think is the difference between "worldly" wisdom and "Godly" wisdom?

When faced with a "challenge," which wisdom do you feel will benefit you the most? Why?

James 1:5 says God gives wisdom generously to all who ask. What does the generosity of God mean to you?

NOTES *EXTRA SPACE FOR SECTION 2 REFLECTION, SERMON NOTES, AND OTHERS

PRAYER REQUEST

Abba Father, let the words that come from our mouth be words of wisdom from Your heart. We are so grateful that we can speak words of life, peace and joy to those around us. In Jesus Name. Amen.

PERSONAL	OTHERS

AFFIRMATION & GRATITUDE

1.

2.

3.

4.

THINGS ON MY HEART

HIGHLIGHTS

TEACH ME | GUIDE ME

FILL YOU WITH ALL JOY
AND PEACE IN BELIEVING,
SO THAT BY THE POWER
OF THE HOLY SPIRIT YOU
MAY ABOUND IN HOPE.

ROMANS 15:13

OVERFLOWING WITH HOPE ROM. 15:13

Hope is a powerful force. A mother waiting for a child to be healed, a man hoping to provide for his children, a couple waiting for a child to be born. The world around us is looking for hope. However, without God, there is no lasting hope, especially if our hope is misplaced in the things or systems of this world. There is only one place we find overflowing hope: from The God of Hope. This God fills us with all joy and peace as we trust Him.

REFLECTION

Have we ever had the feeling when all hope was lost? How did that feel?

Our Heavenly Father gives us overflowing hope when we trust in Him. Why is it difficult to trust God?

Reflect on where that started and ask God to heal you so you can begin to trust Him again. God's ways are higher than our ways. How does that help heal our hearts?

NOTES *EXTRA SPACE FOR SECTION 2 REFLECTION, SERMON NOTES, AND OTHERS

PRAYER REQUEST

Gracious Father, thank You for filling us with all joy and peace in believing, making us abound in hope by the power of The Holy Spirit. In Jesus Name. Amen.

PERSONAL	OTHERS

AFFIRMATION
& GRATITUDE

1.

2.

3.

4.

THINGS ON MY HEART

HIGHLIGHTS

TEACH ME | GUIDE ME

FOR YOU DID NOT RECEIVE THE SPIRIT OF SLAVERY TO FALL BACK INTO FEAR, BUT YOU HAVE RECEIVED THE

AS SONS, BY WHOM WE CRY, "ABBA! FATHER!"

ROMANS 8:15

SPIRIT OF ADOPTION

ROMANS 8:15

The day we received Christ into our hearts is the day we received The Holy Spirit. One of The Holy Spirit's primary purposes is to free us from being slaves to sin. But it does not stop there. The Holy Spirit is also in us to remind us daily that we are sons and daughters of God. We are part of God's family and are given the high privilege of calling God "Abba Father". This privilege is only given to the children of God, who are filled by The Holy Spirit.

____

____

REFLECTION

Have you ever felt that you are all alone in this world and no one really cares? The good news is God cares! He has also made you His child. How does that make you feel?

____

____

____

Why is it so important to know that we are God's children?

____

____

____

When you have doubts about your sonship (or daughtership), you can call on the sweet Holy Spirit living in you. He wants to be your best friend. How does that change everything?

____

____

____

NOTES

*EXTRA SPACE FOR SECTION 2 REFLECTION, SERMON NOTES, AND OTHERS

PRAYER REQUEST

Abba Father, thank You for giving me the sweet Holy Spirit to be my best friend. I am part of Your great family. I am always loved and never alone. In Jesus Name. Amen.

PERSONAL	OTHERS

AFFIRMATION
& GRATITUDE

1.
2.
3.
4.

THINGS ON MY HEART

HIGHLIGHTS

TEACH ME | GUIDE ME

AND HE SAID TO THEM, "COME AWAY BY YOURSELVES TO A DESOLATE PLACE AND REST A WHILE." FOR MANY WERE COMING AND GOING, AND

they had no leisure even to eat

MARK 6:31

THE VALUE OF STILLNESS PART 1

Do you feel the need to stay busy or keep your mind occupied all the time? Can you think of ways to pause and give yourself some space for rest? It could be even just being still in your car or going for a walk. If stepping away is impossible in your day, you can find ways to create stillness amidst your regular flow.

REFLECTION

What is the first thing that comes to mind when you wake up? Do these thoughts give you peace or do they fill you with unhealthy emotions such as stress, fear and anxiety?

Write down how you could start the day with peace and calmness. Think of things you can do differently when you wake up. How does that make you feel?

NOTES *EXTRA SPACE FOR SEC. 2 REFLECTION, SERMON NOTES, AND OTHERS

PRAYER REQUEST

Abba Father, I cast all my cares and burdens on You (name the burdens). I am so glad that You have got my back. I choose to rest, rejoice and give thanks to You in all things, for this is Your will for me in Christ Jesus. Amen.

PERSONAL	OTHERS

AFFIRMATION
& GRATITUDE

1.
2.
3.
4.

THINGS ON MY HEART

HIGHLIGHTS

TEACH ME | GUIDE ME

For God alone
my soul waits
in silence;

FROM HIM
COMES MY
SALVATION.

PSALM 62:1

SPIRITUAL INTERVENTION PART 2

Our first point of awareness is how difficult it is to be still and silent, even for a moment. When we attempt to stop and realize that we cannot, it unveils the areas where we need Holy Spirit intervention! The Spirit helps reveal the mystery of the source of why we feel tired and discontent. If we find it challenging to rest, might we imply that God cannot accomplish His work without our assistance?

REFLECTION

Do you truly trust God to take care of you?

Is there something in the past that has affected your trust in Him?

If you could write to Him, what would you write? Feel free to write anything, small or big, and make peace with Him in your heart.

NOTES

PRAYER REQUEST

Father, thank You for giving me the Spirit of truth who helps me rest in You. Help me be still and know that You are God. In Jesus Name. Amen.

PERSONAL	OTHERS

AFFIRMATION
& GRATITUDE

1.
2.
3.
4.

THINGS ON MY HEART

HIGHLIGHTS

TEACH ME | GUIDE ME

AND KNOCK. IF ANYONE HEARS MY VOICE AND OPENS THE DOOR, I WILL COME IN TO HIM AND EAT WITH HIM, AND HE WITH ME.

REVELATION 3:20

A HEARTFELT CONVERSATION REV. 3:20

Prayer is not a privilege for the religious or a chosen few. Prayer is simply a heartfelt conversation between Daddy God and His child. Child of God, He wants to talk with you. Even now, as you read these words, He gently knocks on the door of your heart. Open it. Welcome him in, and let the conversation begin.

REFLECTION

Have you yearned to speak to Father God and felt you could not speak to Him? Why do you think you've felt that way?

At times, we might feel that the sacrifice of Jesus on the cross for our sins is insufficient. Why do you think this feeling arises?

NOTES

PRAYER REQUEST

Dear Father, our door is open. Come in, let the conversation begin. In Jesus Name. Amen.

PERSONAL	OTHERS

AFFIRMATION & GRATITUDE

1.
2.
3.
4.

THINGS ON MY HEART

HIGHLIGHTS

TEACH ME | GUIDE ME

FOR WE ARE HIS WORKMANSHIP, CREATED IN CHRIST JESUS FOR

WHICH GOD PREPARED BEFOREHAND, THAT WE SHOULD WALK IN THEM.

EPHESIANS 2:10

GOOD WORKS EPHESIANS 2:10

Our spirit man became alive when we received Christ as Lord and Savior. We are a new creation with a new purpose. The Bible calls it good works. Good works are anything and everything we do to glorify God. In a bigger sense, worship is not just singing songs in church; worship is a lifestyle. A lifestyle of glorifying God in every area of our lives, including our jobs, studies, families, relationships; which is good works!

___

___

___

REFLECTION

William Carey, the renowned Baptist missionary to India said this, "Missions exist because worship doesn't". This statement gives us the basis of missions. Do you agree with this statement? How does it change your perspective and definition of worship?

___

___

___

___

___

Worship is not just singing songs. What comes to mind when we see worship as a lifestyle?

___

___

___

___

___

NOTES

PRAYER REQUEST

Abba Father, thank You for revealing to us our mission. Help us not just sing songs about You but let our lives tell Your story. Show us how to truly worship You through our good works. In Jesus Name. Amen.

PERSONAL	OTHERS

AFFIRMATION
& GRATITUDE

1.
2.
3.
4.

THINGS ON MY HEART

HIGHLIGHTS

TEACH ME | GUIDE ME

The heavens declare

THE GLORY OF GOD,
AND THE SKY ABOVE
PROCLAIMS HIS
HANDIWORK.

PSALM 19:1

PARTNERS IN THE KINGDOM

PSALM 19:1

Our Father has given us the wonderful privilege of advancing His Kingdom here on Earth as it is in heaven. He invites us to partner with Him in introducing His marvelous love to all around us. And just as we can learn to think as God thinks, we can also learn how to talk as He talks. Let every breath within us speak of His marvelous love to all of creation.

REFLECTION

Have you been to a place that displayed God's breathtaking creation? How did that make you feel?

Have you ever felt the need to share that experience with someone?

What do you feel when you think about God's love? Why is it so important to you and others?

NOTES

PRAYER REQUEST

Abba Father, thank You for filling our lungs with Your breath this morning. As we breathe in, help us pour out Your praise to those around us and all of creation. In Jesus Name. Amen.

PERSONAL	OTHERS

AFFIRMATION
& GRATITUDE

1.

2.

3.

4.

THINGS ON MY HEART

HIGHLIGHTS

TEACH ME | GUIDE ME

KEEP YOUR HEART
WITH ALL VIGILANCE,
FOR FROM IT

flow the springs of life

PROVERBS 4:23

CHAIN REACTION

PROVERBS 4:23

Filling our thoughts with our Father's Word is where it all begins. Whatever thoughts and words we keep in our minds will eventually find their way out through our mouths. Today, let's hide His Word in our hearts, so that at the opportune time, the appropriate words will be released. Romans 12:2 says, " be transformed by the entire renewal of your mind." When we transform our mind with God's Word, we set off a chain reaction that also transforms our mouths, moods, attitudes, actions, and every other area of our lives.

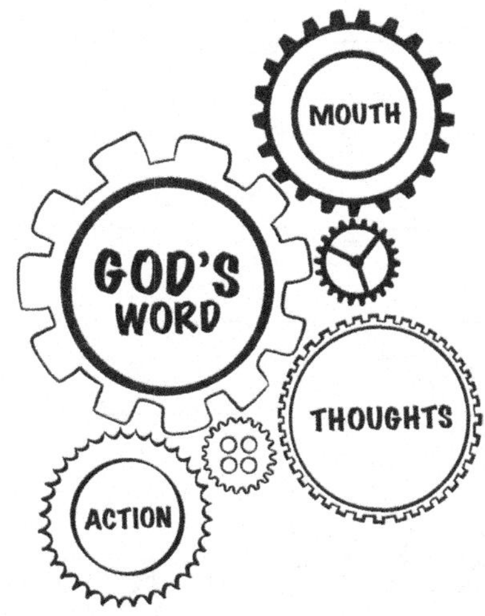

REFLECTION

Why is storing God's Word in our hearts so important?

Why does our mind need to think as God thinks?

Have you ever been taken by surprise when you shared the exact scripture someone needed? Or when someone spoke the exact word you needed? How did it make you feel?

NOTES

PRAYER REQUEST

Abba Father, we let not steadfast love and faithfulness forsake us; we bind them around our neck; write them on the tablet of our hearts. So we will find favor and good success in the sight of God and man. In Jesus Name. Amen. (based on Proverbs 3:3-4).

PERSONAL	OTHERS

AFFIRMATION
& GRATITUDE

1.

2.

3.

THINGS ON MY HEART

HIGHLIGHTS

TEACH ME | GUIDE ME

BUT THE HELPER, THE HOLY SPIRIT, WHOM THE FATHER WILL SEND IN MY NAME, HE

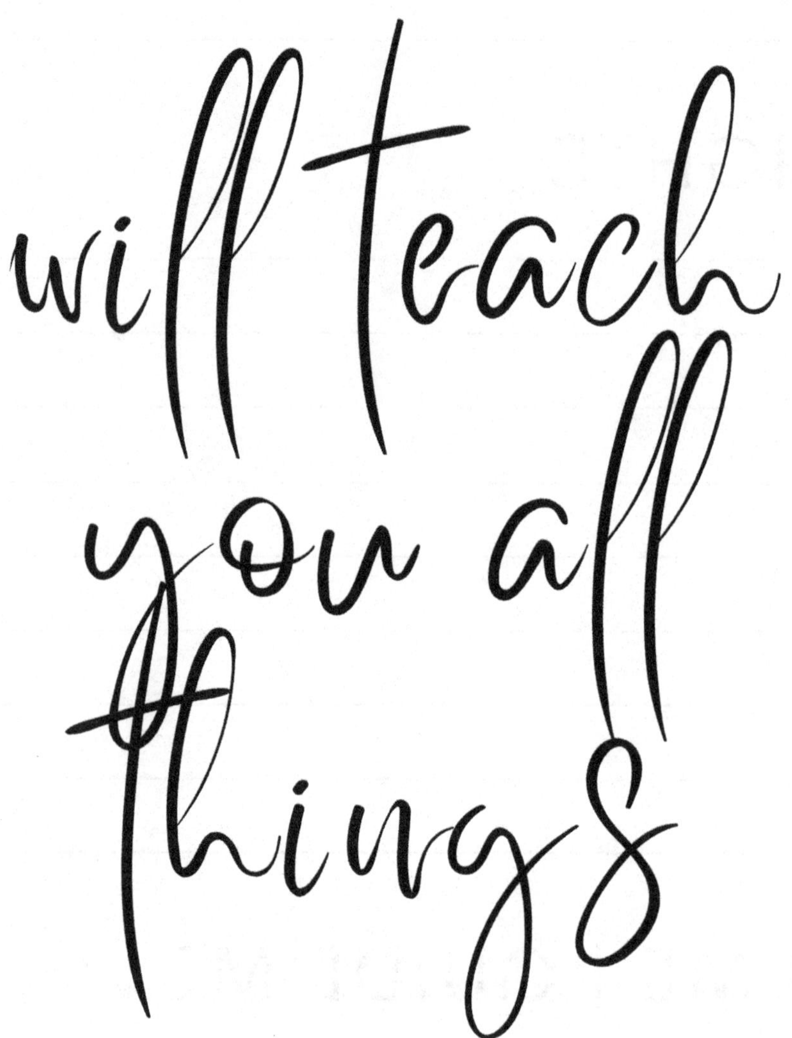

AND BRING TO YOUR REMEMBRANCE ALL THAT I HAVE SAID TO YOU.

JOHN 14:26

THE PIVOTAL DAY JOHN 14:26

The Day of Pentecost was one of the most significant events in history, as it marked the day of "the coming of the Holy Spirit." Jesus had prepared the disciples for this momentous day. Throughout the Bible, the revelation of the Holy Spirit "dwelling in us" had been building up... (Joel 2:28–29, Luke 3:16, Acts 4:8, etc)

REFLECTION

Have you ever felt overwhelmed by a circumstance or news? How did it make you feel?

Did you wish there were someone to provide comfort or guidance? Why did you feel that way? It is interesting to note that The Holy Spirit in the original Greek language is defined as counselor and comforter.

NOTES

PRAYER REQUEST

Father God, thank You for the honor and privilege of making us the dwelling place of The Holy Spirit here on earth. In Jesus Name. Amen.

PERSONAL	OTHERS

AFFIRMATION
& GRATITUDE

1.

2.

3.

4.

THINGS ON MY HEART

HIGHLIGHTS

TEACH ME | GUIDE ME

THE TONGUE HAS
THE POWER OF

life and death,

AND THOSE WHO
LOVE IT WILL EAT
ITS FRUIT.

PROVERBS 18:21

LIFE AND DEATH PART 1

The connection between what we think and what we say is stronger than many realize. We've heard the phrase, "Think before you speak." However, much of what we think sometimes falls out of our mouths with no forethought as to how it will sound or who it may hurt. Other times, we meditate on something so frequently that we can't help eventually saying it, even if it's something we don't want others to know we're thinking.

REFLECTION

Why are words spoken out of our mouths important to our lives and the ones around us?

Can we confront evil and yet bring life through our words?

NOTES

PRAYER REQUEST

Abba Father, thank You for filling our mouths with Your praises today. Help us to have wisdom when to speak, and to speak life giving and encouraging words. In Jesus Name. Amen.

PERSONAL	OTHERS

AFFIRMATION & GRATITUDE

1.

2.

3.

4.

THINGS ON MY HEART

HIGHLIGHTS

TEACH ME | GUIDE ME

ANXIETY IN A MAN'S HEART WEIGHS HIM DOWN, BUT

a good word makes him glad.

PROVERBS 12:25

WORDS OF POWER PART 2

The truth is, words affect our lives and those around us. They are containers filled with power. Power to bless or curse, build up or tear down, encourage or discourage hearts. Let's ask The Holy Spirit to help us use our words wisely.

REFLECTION

Can you remember a time you were encouraged by a word from someone? How did that make you feel?

What is a scripture that often encourages you? Why does it encourage you?

NOTES

PRAYER REQUEST

Abba Father, You spoke kindly and lovingly over us even when we did not deserve it. Your loving kindness is better than life. Thank You for giving us The Helper to help us use our words wisely. In Jesus Name. Amen.

PERSONAL	OTHERS

AFFIRMATION
& GRATITUDE

1.

2.

3.

4.

THINGS ON MY HEART

HIGHLIGHTS

TEACH ME | GUIDE ME

AND DO NOT GET DRUNK WITH WINE, FOR THAT IS DEBAUCHERY, BUT

ADDRESSING ONE ANOTHER IN PSALMS AND HYMNS AND SPIRITUAL SONGS, SINGING AND MAKING MELODY TO THE LORD WITH YOUR HEART.

EPHESIANS 5:18–19

TUNED TO THE SPIRIT EPHESIANS 5:18-19

After we are saved, we are to be filled and continue to be "filled with the Spirit" daily! The Holy Spirit inspires us to sing and make melodies to The Lord, which helps us keep our faith, hope and love alive.

REFLECTION

What emotions arise when a song or Psalm moves you?

How did you feel before the song started?

Why do you think your emotions changed after hearing the song?

NOTES

PRAYER REQUEST

Holy Spirit, thank You for helping us drink deeply by making melody in our hearts unto The Father. Thank You for keeping our faith alive! In Jesus Name. Amen.

PERSONAL	OTHERS

AFFIRMATION
& GRATITUDE

1.

2.

3.

4.

THINGS ON MY HEART

HIGHLIGHTS

TEACH ME | GUIDE ME

In the beginning,

GOD CREATED
THE HEAVENS
AND THE EARTH.

GENESIS 1:1

BEYOND COINCIDENCE GENESIS 1:1

From the very beginning, the Bible assumes the existence of God. "In the beginning, God created the heavens and the earth" (Genesis 1:1). That anyone could look at the wonder of the universe and call it a "coincidence" is unimaginable.

REFLECTION

There are opinions that suggest we are here by chance and that our existence is a coincidence. How does that make you feel?

Each of us has a privilege and, along with it, a responsibility over God's creation. How does this realization alter the way you perceive yourself?

NOTES

PRAYER REQUEST

Daddy God, we are so grateful for the privilege of being called daughters and sons by the Creator of the universe and to call You, Abba Father. In Jesus Name. Amen.

PERSONAL	OTHERS

AFFIRMATION
& GRATITUDE

1.
2.
3.
4.

THINGS ON MY HEART

HIGHLIGHTS

TEACH ME | GUIDE ME

BLESSED BE THE GOD AND FATHER OF OUR LORD JESUS CHRIST, WHO HAS BLESSED US IN CHRIST WITH

every spiritual blessing in the heavenly places.

EPHESIANS 1:3

SPIRITUAL BLESSING

EPHESIANS 1:3

What an incredible promise! Something powerful happened when we opened our hearts to Jesus, our Prince of Peace. Our Heavenly Father has blessed us not just with one or two, but with EVERY spiritual blessing in the heavenly places. This isn't something He is going to do; it's something He has already DONE.

REFLECTION

Reflect on these spiritual blessings that you already HAVE in Christ Jesus. Hint: it is related to your position and identity in Christ when you received Him into your heart.

How do you feel about God and His promises to you?

NOTES

PRAYER REQUEST

Abba Father thank You for blessing us in Christ, with every spiritual blessing in the heavenly places. In Jesus Name. Amen.

PERSONAL	OTHERS

AFFIRMATION
& GRATITUDE

1.
2.
3.
4.

THINGS ON MY HEART

HIGHLIGHTS

TEACH ME | GUIDE ME

FOR HE IS
LIKE ONE
WHO IS

inwardly calculating

PROVERBS 23:7

INNER CONVERSATION PART 1

Do we give thought to our inner conversations? This may sound funny; however, learning to take inventory of our thoughts regularly is essential to having a good life. Instead of being "unthinking" people, we can train our minds to pause and "give thought" to what's going on in our minds. Whatever is going on internally, whether positive or otherwise, will eventually find its way out and shape our destiny. Let's choose to align our minds and hearts with Daddy God's.

REFLECTION

Do you think your inner conversation is important? We see athletes and characters from the Bible do it all the time.

Why is it important to align our inner conversation with Daddy God?

What do you think happens when our inner conversation is aligned with God's?

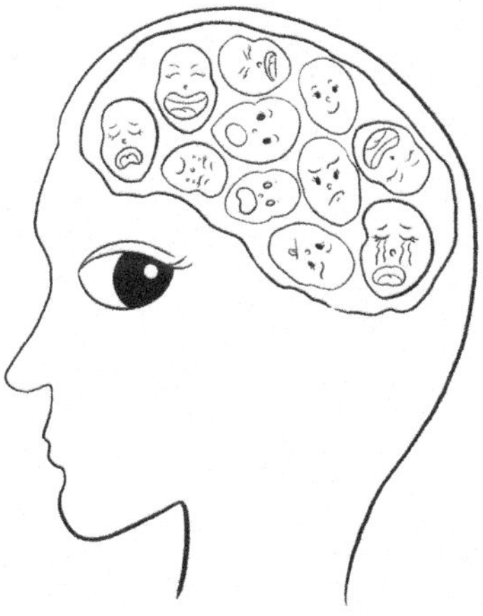

NOTES

PRAYER REQUEST

Abba Father, thank You for Your precious Word that helps us align our thoughts with Yours today. In Jesus Name. Amen.

PERSONAL	OTHERS

AFFIRMATION
& GRATITUDE

1.
2.
3.
4.

THINGS ON MY HEART

HIGHLIGHTS

TEACH ME | GUIDE ME

WE DESTROY ARGUMENTS AND EVERY LOFTY OPINION RAISED AGAINST THE KNOWLEDGE OF GOD, AND

take every thought captive

TO OBEY CHRIST.

2 CORINTHIANS 10:5

REBUILDING NEW PATHWAYS PART 2

We don't have to sit by passively and let the enemy build pathways of destructive thoughts in our minds. Instead, we can learn to recognize them and, with God's help, rebuild constructive pathways that build confidence and faith.

REFLECTION

Do you find yourself thinking of the worst possible scenario when you hear something troubling? Would you consider yourself an optimist or a pessimist?

Do you have trouble sleeping, repeatedly mulling over something hurtful or troubling that has happened? Why do you think this happens?

Why is it important to reverse these destructive patterns of thinking? When do you think you started thinking this way?

NOTES

PRAYER REQUEST

Abba Father, how we delight in Your Word. Help us build new pathways of love, joy and peace through the power and leading of The HOLY SPIRIT. In Jesus Name. Amen.

PERSONAL	OTHERS

AFFIRMATION
& GRATITUDE

1.

2.

3.

4.

THINGS ON MY HEART

HIGHLIGHTS

TEACH ME | GUIDE ME

Fear not,
for I am
with you

; BE NOT DISMAYED,
FOR I AM YOUR GOD; I
WILL STRENGTHEN
YOU, I WILL HELP YOU,
I WILL UPHOLD YOU
WITH MY RIGHTEOUS
RIGHT HAND.

ISAIAH 41:10

MONKEY MIND PART 3

Often, learning to tame the mind can be like trying to tame a wild animal. When we first begin making an effort to control our own thinking, attempting to replace the negative thoughts with positive ones, it can sometimes be challenging, and we might feel as though we'll never succeed. But don't give up. God is for us!

REFLECTION

Have you tried to tame your thoughts but found it difficult and given up? Why? Remember, God is for you.

There are people around you who want to help. How does that make you feel? Why do you feel that way?

NOTES

PRAYER REQUEST

Abba Father, we are more than conquerors through Christ who loves us. We bring captive every thought to the obedience of Christ and the Word of God. In Jesus Name. Amen.

PERSONAL	OTHERS

AFFIRMATION & GRATITUDE

1.

2.

3.

4.

THINGS ON MY HEART

HIGHLIGHTS

TEACH ME | GUIDE ME

God is spirit,

AND THOSE WHO WORSHIP HIM MUST WORSHIP IN SPIRIT AND TRUTH.

JOHN 4:24

WORSHIP IN SPIRIT JOHN 4:24

We are uniquely created to worship God in spirit. This verse highlights the difference between us and all of God's creation. The difference is that we are not only body and soul but also spirit. This is what sets us apart from all other creatures.

REFLECTION

Worship involves connecting with God. However, God is a spirit, and we can only worship Him with the help of the Holy Spirit. Have you ever had trouble worshipping? Why do you think it was challenging? How did that make you feel?

Worship serves as a connection to God. Why is this connection important?

How did you feel after a fulfilling worship session? What made it a positive experience?

NOTES

PRAYER REQUEST

Daddy God, thank You for setting us apart from all of Your creation and giving us a spirit like Yours, created to worship and love You. We love you, Daddy. In Jesus Name. Amen.

PERSONAL	OTHERS

AFFIRMATION & GRATITUDE

1.
2.
3.
4.

THINGS ON MY HEART

HIGHLIGHTS

TEACH ME | GUIDE ME

If we confess our sins

HE IS FAITHFUL AND JUST TO FORGIVE US OUR SINS AND TO CLEANSE US FROM ALL UNRIGHTEOUSNESS.

1 JOHN 1:9

THE POWER OF THE BLOOD 1 JOHN 1:9

Sometimes, we feel we must "pay" for our sins by feeling bad about ourselves. If it was a "small" sin, we might feel guilty for a day or so. If it was something "significant," it might last an entire week! We must realize that Jesus paid the price for all our sins and guilt. When we sin, the greatest thing we can do is confess it to the Lord, receive His forgiveness, and move forward (1 John 1:9). We can leave the guilt behind!

REFLECTION

What emotions fill your heart when you remember the cross where Jesus died to pay for all our sins and guilt? How does that help you?

Why is it still important to confess our sins if Jesus has already paid for them all? How does it help?

NOTES

PRAYER REQUEST

Thank you, Jesus, for Your precious blood that reminds me that sin no longer has a hold on me or can hold me back. In Jesus Name. Amen.

PERSONAL	OTHERS

AFFIRMATION
& GRATITUDE

1.

2.

3.

4.

THINGS ON MY HEART

HIGHLIGHTS

TEACH ME | GUIDE ME

COME TO ME, ALL WHO
LABOR AND ARE HEAVY
LADEN, AND

I will give you rest.

TAKE MY YOKE UPON YOU, AND
LEARN FROM ME, FOR I AM GENTLE
AND LOWLY IN HEART, AND YOU
WILL FIND REST FOR YOUR SOULS.

MATTHEW 11:28–29

FINDING REST PART 1

We may feel overwhelmed when we see the number of areas needing rest and healing in our lives. The good news is that rest comes not from our works but Christ's finished work on the cross.

REFLECTION

In what areas of our life are we yearning for rest?

Christ has made a way through the cross for rest in those very areas. Let us take a few moments to reflect and write down how God's promises provide us a way of rest in those areas.

NOTES

PRAYER REQUEST

Abba Father, thank You for Christ's finished work on the cross that has made a way for us to have a pathway of rest. We remember that Your grace is sufficient for us, and your strength is made perfect in our weaknesses. In Jesus Name. Amen.

PERSONAL	OTHERS

AFFIRMATION
& GRATITUDE

1.
2.
3.
4.

THINGS ON MY HEART

HIGHLIGHTS

TEACH ME | GUIDE ME

The Lord
is my
shepherd;

I SHALL NOT
WANT.

PSALMS 23:1

SOURCE OF REST PSALMS 23:1

Today, focus on the truth that God is the ultimate source of the rest we long for. When was the last time you allowed yourself to just drink in the reality of who God truly is? Most of our lives are lived acknowledging the importance of God but not truly remembering and focusing on His story.

REFLECTION

Father God is our source of rest. How does that make you feel?

Write down scriptures or songs of His faithfulness that come to mind. Even a line or verse is great!

NOTES

PRAYER REQUEST

Abba Father, thank You for Your unfailing love. Thank You for using every season of our lives to show us Who You really are. In Jesus Name. Amen.

PERSONAL	OTHERS

AFFIRMATION
& GRATITUDE

1.

2.

3.

4.

THINGS ON MY HEART

HIGHLIGHTS

TEACH ME | GUIDE ME

But our citizenship

IS IN HEAVEN, AND FROM IT WE AWAIT A SAVIOR, THE LORD JESUS CHRIST

PHILIPPIANS 3:20

CITIZENS OF HEAVEN

PHILIPPIANS 3:20

We are given a new spiritual citizenship when we receive Christ as our Lord and Savior. It is not unlike our earthly citizenship. We enjoy all the benefits of heaven and can look forward to every life experience with great hope. Each time we go through tumultuous times, we can fix our eyes on the hope within us and the eternity we have with our Heavenly Father.

REFLECTION

We are citizens of heaven. What comes to mind when you reflect on that?

Instead of feeling overwhelmed and defeated, we can live as overcomers. Why is that important?

How does that change the way you see challenges now?

NOTES

PRAYER REQUEST

Abba Father, thank You for making me a citizen of heaven. Instead of being overwhelmed, could you show me the way of an overcomer? In Jesus Name. Amen.

PERSONAL	OTHERS

AFFIRMATION
& GRATITUDE

1.
2.
3.
4.

THINGS ON MY HEART

HIGHLIGHTS

TEACH ME | GUIDE ME

Behold, I am doing a new thing;

NOW IT SPRINGS FORTH,
DO YOU NOT PERCEIVE
IT? I WILL MAKE A WAY IN
THE WILDERNESS AND
RIVERS IN THE DESERT.

ISAIAH 43:19

A RENEWED MIND

ISAIAH 43:19

Our minds are powerful, and our thoughts have the ability to affect our performance in every area of life. In fact, our lives cannot go forward if our minds are going backward!

BACKWARD THINKING

FORWARD THINKING

REFLECTION

Would you consider yourself a forward-thinking or backward-thinking person? Why do you feel that way about yourself?

Why do you think that being forward-thinking is important?

Do you think there's a difference between a "worldly" way versus a Godly way of forward-thinking? What do you think is the difference, and which do you consider better? Why? In what way do you believe God's Word helps foster forward-thinking?

NOTES

PRAYER REQUEST

Holy Spirit, thank You for helping us to forget the former things and reach forward into the wonderful destiny You have prepared for us. In Jesus Name. Amen.

PERSONAL	OTHERS

AFFIRMATION
& GRATITUDE

1.
2.
3.
4.

THINGS ON MY HEART

HIGHLIGHTS

TEACH ME | GUIDE ME

THEN KING DAVID WENT IN AND SAT BEFORE THE LORD AND SAID, "WHO AM I, O LORD GOD, AND WHAT IS MY HOUSE, THAT YOU HAVE

brought me thus far?

2 SAMUEL 7:18

SHAPING DESTINY

2 SAMUEL 7:18

What we choose to remember and forget determines our destiny. When King David was troubled, he chose to remember the great victories he had before, and it increased his faith. In the same way, we can choose to reflect upon all the great things God has done for us and the "victories" we've achieved in the past. As we do that, it will strengthen our faith and provide us with confidence for the days ahead.

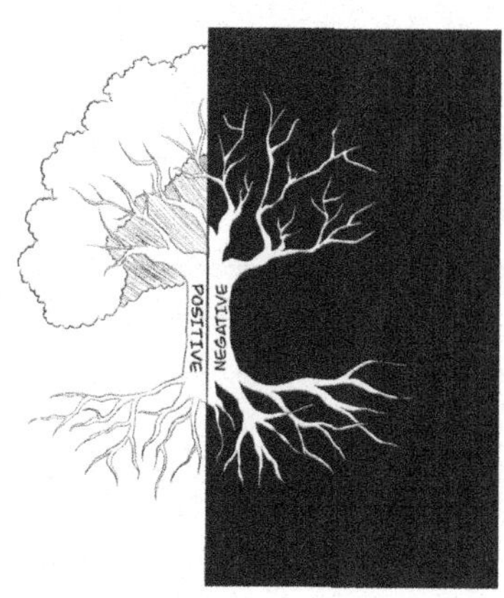

REFLECTION

Why is it so important to remember the great victories God has given to us in the past?

Why is sharing testimonies about the past important? In what ways does it help you and others?

How do you think God feels when you share your past victories? Is it important how others may or may not feel about your testimonies?

NOTES

PRAYER REQUEST

Daddy God, we are grateful for how You saved and blessed us. Thank You for carrying us all these years. You never left nor forsaken us, carrying us through every storm and giving us victory. In Jesus Name. Amen.

PERSONAL	OTHERS

AFFIRMATION
& GRATITUDE

1.
2.
3.
4.

THINGS ON MY HEART

HIGHLIGHTS

TEACH ME | GUIDE ME

THEN THE LORD GOD FORMED THE MAN OF DUST FROM THE GROUND AND

breathed into his nostrils the breath of life, and

THE MAN BECAME A LIVING CREATURE.

GENESIS 2:7

CREATED FOR ETERNITY PART 1

God breathed His own breath (Spirit) into our lungs. Imagine that! God made no other creature like us. We are spirits, eternal beings made for both this earth and eternity. Our spirits and souls are the innermost parts of our being. They contain the very breath of God's life and are the seat of God's presence. Our spirit is an eternal existence and being. God is Spirit, the embodiment of eternal life.

REFLECTION

Have you ever had the feeling that you were made for something bigger?

The eternal spirit lives in us, and we were made to live eternally with God. How does that realization make you feel?

The world is temporary and passing away. How does our perspective change when we see ourselves as eternal beings in relation to our daily struggles?

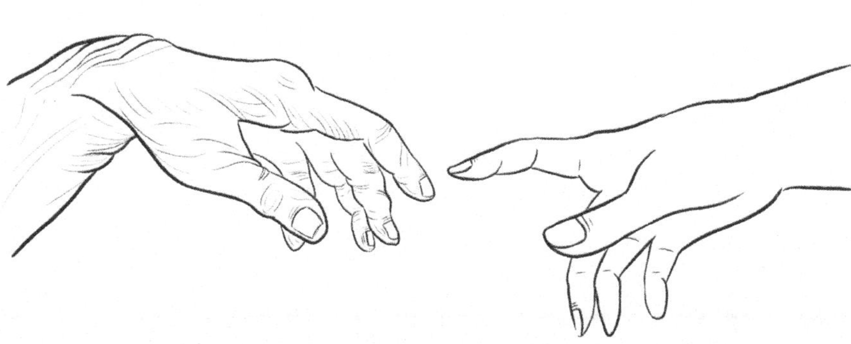

NOTES

PRAYER REQUEST

Abba Father, You are eternal. Thank You for breathing that same eternal breath of Your Spirit in us to live and fellowship with You forever. In Jesus Name. Amen.

PERSONAL	OTHERS

AFFIRMATION
& GRATITUDE

1.

2.

3.

4.

THINGS ON MY HEART

HIGHLIGHTS

TEACH ME | GUIDE ME

NOW JESUS WAS PRAYING IN A CERTAIN PLACE, AND WHEN HE FINISHED, ONE OF HIS DISCIPLES SAID TO HIM,"

Lord, teach us to pray,

AS JOHN TAUGHT HIS DISCIPLES."

LUKE 11:1

THE HEART OF THE FATHER LUKE 11:1

This much is sure: Abba Father desires to teach us to pray. Let us remove any image that He is glaring at us from a distance with crossed arms and a frown, waiting for us to get our prayer life together. It is just the opposite. His arms are extended in love, and He is waiting to receive us and hear our voice.

REFLECTION

Have you ever struggled to put words together in prayer, especially in front of others? Why do you feel that way?

The only one who needs to hear our prayers is Daddy God. How does that make you feel?

NOTES

PRAYER REQUEST

Abba Father, thank you for the promise that you will draw near to us as we draw near to You. Thank You that You are an ever-present help at all times of need. Help us remove any image that does not reflect Who You are. Thank You for being our good, good Father. In Jesus Name. Amen.

PERSONAL	OTHERS

AFFIRMATION
& GRATITUDE

1.

2.

3.

THINGS ON MY HEART

HIGHLIGHTS

TEACH ME | GUIDE ME

BROTHERS, I DO NOT CONSIDER THAT I HAVE MADE IT MY OWN. BUT ONE THING I DO:

forgetting what lies behind

AND STRAINING FORWARD TO WHAT LIES AHEAD.

PHILIPPIANS 3:13

LETTING GO PHILIPPIANS 3:13

Thinking and dwelling on past hurts or mistakes can actually cause us to relive the pain and prevent us from moving forward. In this verse, the apostle Paul discusses moving toward spiritual maturity in Christ and the importance of "forgetting what lies behind." Why is it so important to shake off the past? If we spend today thinking and dwelling on yesterday's mistakes, then we'll never make the progress we desire because guilt and condemnation will steal our energy!

REFLECTION

Holding on to the past can be likened to a colossal burden tied to our backs. How does it feel when you release your burdens to Daddy God?

Why is it so important to let go of past experiences of pain and failures?

In what situations are pain and hurts important to be remembered? How does looking ahead help you?

NOTES

PRAYER REQUEST

Abba Father, we fix our eyes on You. Point out to us the good that lies ahead. In Jesus Name. Amen.

PERSONAL	OTHERS

AFFIRMATION
& GRATITUDE

1.
2.
3.
4.

THINGS ON MY HEART

HIGHLIGHTS

TEACH ME | GUIDE ME

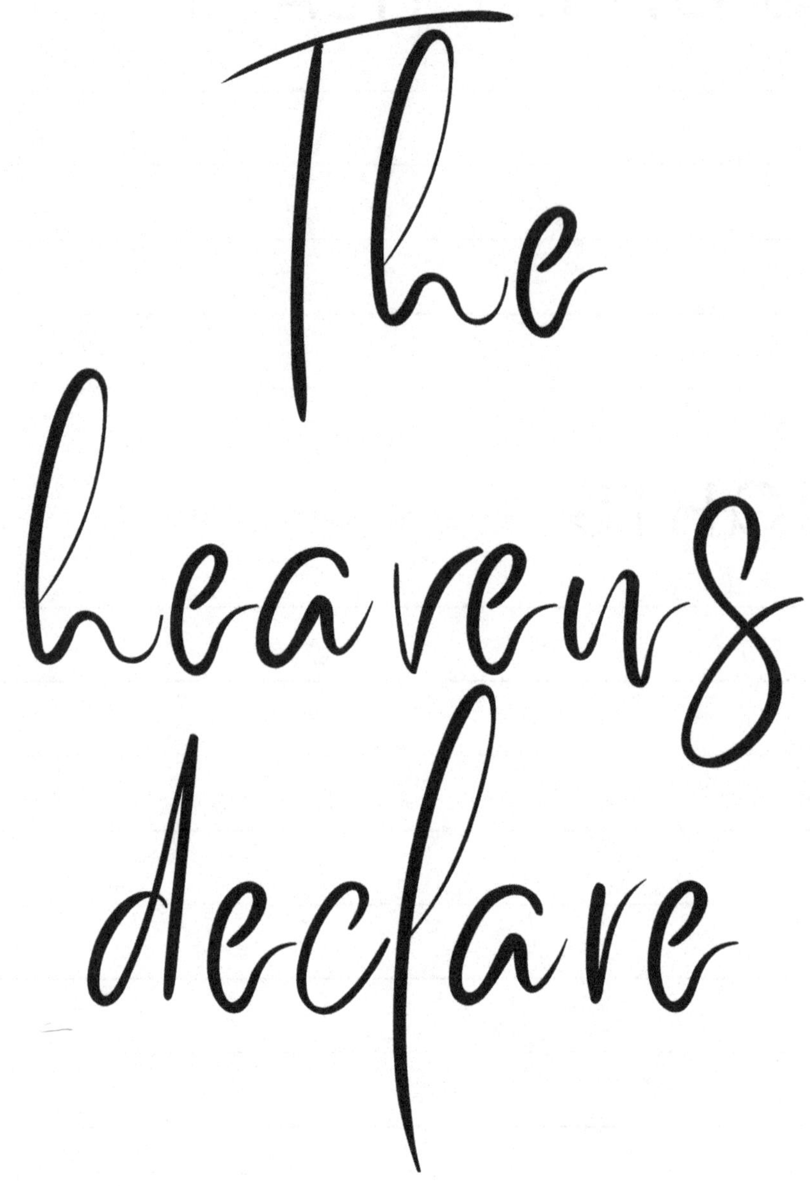

THE GLORY OF GOD,
AND THE SKY ABOVE
PROCLAIMS HIS
HANDIWORK.

PSALM 19:1

UNVEILING GOD'S VOICE

PSALM 19:1

Everything that exists gives evidence of God's speech. The uniqueness of our fingerprints, the roar of a tropical thunderstorm, the precision of geese formation in flight, and the bubbling of a mountain stream. These miracles and many more bear testimony to the existence of a brilliant, wise and tireless God who is always speaking.

REFLECTION

We often ask ourselves, "How can we hear the voice of God?" Unlike us, God is not limited to one way or certain moments of communication. God wants to speak to us more than we are often willing to listen. How does that change how you feel about hearing God's voice?

How does that change the way we listen to God?

God speaks through everything around us. Why is this truth important to us?

NOTES

PRAYER REQUEST

Daddy God, thank You for giving us fresh ears to hear Your voice. Help us be sensitive to every little way You speak to us. Thank You for filling us with the comfort and assurance of Your voice. In Jesus Name. Amen.

PERSONAL	OTHERS

AFFIRMATION
& GRATITUDE

1.
2.
3.
4.

THINGS ON MY HEART

HIGHLIGHTS

TEACH ME | GUIDE ME

NOTES

1.

2.

3.

4.

5.

6.

7.

NOTES

1.
2.
3.
4.
5.
6.
7.

Made in the USA
Monee, IL
23 June 2024